Forest Friends

by Cat Jenkins

First Edition

ISBN 979-8-89297-191-1

95 Percent Group LLC
475 Half Day Road, Suite 350 ▪ Lincolnshire, IL 60069
847-499-8200
95percentgroup.com
Printed in the United States of America.

10 9 8 7 6 5 4 3 2 1
R1.09.25

Table of Contents

The Explorer's Word Log

Let's dive into some key vocabulary words.

Chapter 1

chatter	(verb): to close (teeth) together quickly, again and again, usually because of the cold
cloak	(noun): covering that hides whatever is underneath it
foe	(noun): enemy
seek	(verb): to look for
tropical	(adjective): having a hot and humid climate

Chapter 2

lay claim to	(verb): to take
faint	(adjective): hard to notice
hooves	(noun): plural of "hoof," the hard covering over a moose's foot
resourceful	(adjective): good at solving problems

Chapter 3

froth	(noun): a group of small bubbles
temperate	(adjective): having a mild climate that is not very hot or very cold
thrive	(verb): to grow or do well

Chapter 4

Chapter 5

Chapter 6

Chapter 1

Forest Friends

Forest Friends
Predictable Vowel Teams

ee

feet	sleep
freeze	sweet
green	teeth
seek	tree

igh

bright	night
high	right
light	sight
might	

oa

cloak	soak
coat	toast
road	

oe

foe
toe

High-Frequency Words

Regular

color	far	know
even	food	south
every	grow	year

Irregular

from	some
many	their

Challenge Words

bathing	farther	humid	matter	season	tropical
different	forest	Japanese	prepare	treetop	

95 Percent Group

Storyshares

From the desert, which
has sand as far as you
can see, we go right to the
forest.

The forest is light, but
it is not as bright as the

desert, where you toast in
the sun. The forest is green,
but there are many kinds of
forests.

Some in the north can
freeze and make your teeth

chatter.

Some in the south soak in hot and humid rain, but still, under the cloak of night, might make you wish for a coat.

A forest in the north is cold much of the year. The plants know that their time is short, so they sleep more than they wake.

If you take a road south,

it will lead to warm forests
where it is sweet to have

the best of all four seasons.
Here you will find plants
that grow in spring and
summer, and trees that
dress in fall colors.

If your feet take you

even farther south, there
are much warmer forests
where you can get a sight of
tropical plants.

The animals here seek a
home high in the vines and

treetops. The forest might
get a rain bath every night.

No matter how different
they are, all forests have a
lot of trees that grow side
by side.

Land can be flat or have
sand, a lake, or many hills,
but there must be trees for
it to be a forest.

Each kind of forest is
home to different kinds of

animals. They might fly, swim, or hang from a tree by their toes. Each animal has a set of gifts that prepare it to find food and stay safe from foes.

Let's take a look at how
the forest is home to many.

Chapter 2

The Moose

The Moose
Predictable Vowel Teams

ai
air	daily	gain	sail
claim	faint	rain	tail

au
pause

aw
crawl	thaw
jaw	

ay
bay	may
lay	way

oi
join
noise

oy
toy

High-Frequency Words

Regular
after	even	seven
before	family	
easy	far	

Irregular
again	from	through
among	live	
does	often	

Challenge Words

bear	food	moose	return	winter
biggest	hear	North America	strength	wolf
enemy	hoof	pounds	water	

From jaw to tail, moose are the biggest animals in the deer family, and they even join ranks among the biggest animals that live in North America. A moose

may stand seven feet tall
and may gain as much as
1,800 pounds after birth.
When it comes to size, a
moose can lay claim to a
top spot.

The moose's hooves are wide, and its legs are long. This makes it easy for the moose to sail through a lake or wade through a bay without a misstep. When

there is a thaw and there is
a lot of rain and mud, wide
hooves keep the moose from
slowing to a crawl.

The moose does not need
to hunt or fight for food in

the forest. There is a lot
of food, and the moose is
resourceful. Its daily meal
is twigs, bark, leaves and
shoots from the trees and
shrubs that grow in forests.

A moose's nose and top
lip are made for stripping
leaves and grabbing water
plants.

The moose has sharp
hearing and a keen sense of

smell that forewarns them
of danger. From far away,
they can pick up the faint
smell or noise of an enemy.
The moose will often pause
and prepare to fight if

it senses that a wolf or
a bear hunts it. One hit
from a moose hoof can
make a wolf sail through
the air like a toy!

A moose's thick fur
keeps it warm in winter
before spring makes a
return.

With its size and strength, the moose is made for the way of life in the cold forests of the north.

Just as a camel may close its nose to keep sand out, a moose may close its nose as a way to keep water out. This gains the moose time under water when it **dives as deep as 20 feet** to eat water plants.

🦻)) optional teacher read-aloud

Chapter 3
The Hedgehog

The Hedgehog
Unpredictable Vowel Teams

ie (2 sounds for ie)

field	dried
	lie
	tried

ow (2 sounds for ow)

brown	blow
down	flow
	low
	snow

High-Frequency Words

Regular

first	more
food	south
found	work

Irregular

another	live
does	onto

Challenge Words

Africa	Europe	human	poison	tool
Asia	hair	itself	predator	
central	hedgehog	keratin	temperate	

Down south of the
forests where moose live
are more temperate forests.
Here you can find animals
that thrive in wild lands
where the snow does not

blow as much.

A kind of hedgehog can be found in the temperate fields and forests of Europe, central Asia, and North Africa.

These forests flow with
the food that hedgehogs
like. Here they find bugs,
slugs, snails, toads, snakes,
and frogs. A hedgehog with
boldness can go up a tree to

hunt for bird eggs, too.

A hedgehog is small, brown-gray, and not as fast as a fox or a wolf, but it can use its quills to protect itself from predators. First,

it will stay low and try to run away. If it can't get

away, the hedgehog will
try to ram the foe with its
sharp spines.

If that does not work,
the hedgehog will lie down
and roll into a ball so there

is no way to sink teeth into
it without getting a prickly
blow.

Another hedgehog trick
is to bite on a plant that has
poison or a bad taste. It will

make a froth from the plant
and lick it onto its spines.
Even if the froth is dried, its
bad taste will put a stop to
a predator that goes to bite
the hedgehog.

The hedgehog may be cute, but it does have the tools to stay safe at home in the forest.

Chapter 4

The Sharp-Shinned Hawk

The Sharp-Shinned Hawk
Unpredictable Vowel Teams

ea (2 sounds for ea)

beak	seat	head
each	steal	spread
eat	streak	
feast	weak	
leave		
meal		
meat		
reach		

oo (2 sounds for oo)

choose	good
food	hook
roof	look

High-Frequency Words

Regular

after
below
over

Irregular

above	move	very
from	only	
live	other	

Challenge Words

backyard	hidden	predator	talon
bigger	larger	preferable	temperate
canopy	North America	smallest	undercover
feeder	place	spruce	

Temperate forests make good homes for the birds that choose to live there.

The sharp-shinned hawk is one that finds a place where there are lots of pine,

spruce, and fir trees.

The sharp-shinned hawk
is the smallest hawk in
North America. Its small
size lets it streak after
its food where leaves and

branches grow tightly.

With talons and a beak that can hook and rip, the sharp-shinned hawk likes to feast on the meat of small birds.

Most hawks dive from the sky. But the sharp-shinned

Female sharp-shinned hawks **are bigger** than males. Females choose to feast on larger birds than males do, so they never steal each other's meal.

)) optional teacher read-aloud

hawk will steal over to the
side of the forest, take a
seat, and stay very still. It
will move only its head as it
looks for a bird to get close.
Then it will spread its wings

and strike at its prey. If the
little birds hide, the hawk
will stake out backyard bird
feeders. The hawk will make
a game of it and chase birds
that come to eat. It will

make a meal of birds that are weak or slow.

The sharp-shinned hawk finds pine, spruce, and fir trees preferable for its nest. The forest's canopy, or roof,

must be thick to keep the nest
undercover from predators
who fly above. In the forest
sub-roof, the tree branches
must reach close to each
other to make the nest and its

eggs hidden from foes below.
Small size is not a point
of pride for many animals,
but for the sharp-shinned
hawk, it makes the dense
forest a good home.

Chapter 5

The Jaguar

The Jaguar
Unpredictable Vowel Teams

ou (2 sounds of ou)

clout	touch
found	
out	
pounce	
sound	
trout	

ew (2 sounds of ew)

few	crew
	flew

High-Frequency Words

Regular

even	number
first	upon
more	

Irregular

about	give
also	move
because	of

Challenge Words

climb	itself	lion	shadow	tropic
diverse	jaguar	northern	someone	without
impressive	jungle	rainforest	travel	

Tropical forests host a wider number of animals than northern or temperate forests. The tropics are home to a diverse bunch of animals.

All are impressive, but
few can be found that stand
out like the jaguar.
The first thing you see
when you look at a jaguar
is its fur. The fur looks soft

to touch and has tan spots
ringed with black all over it.
In the dense jungle forest,
the jaguar blends with the
shadows cast by trees and
leaves. These spots let it

go unseen by its prey until
the jaguar is close and can
pounce upon it. The spots
also protect it from the few
predators it has.

In a tropical rainforest,

the jaguar may come
upon a lake, pond, or river
where it can find fish, like
trout. Jaguars are good
swimmers. The jaguar can
even hold its breath under

water so it can hunt those trout.

You may think of the jaguar as a big cat, but it is small next to a lion or tiger. Because of its smaller

size, the jaguar and its crew
are free to move about in
the thick jungle forest with
ease.

The jaguar's paws give it
even more clout in the jungle

forest. With thicker pads
and stronger claws, it can
climb up a tree to protect
itself or to hide so it can
jump upon prey.

The jaguar can swim,

climb, and move without a sound, making the tropical forest its best home.

Chapter 6

The Capybara

The Capybara
Review

Predictable Vowel Teams

keep	seem	might	crawl	noise	cause	play
meet	seen	sight	saw	point		stay
needed	sleep					way
reed	teeth	toe				

Unpredictable Vowel Teams

down	breath	food	pound
growing	each	good	tough
grown	feast		
known	head		
low	mean		
	reach		
	team		

High-Frequency Words

Regular

able	never
know	place
more	

Irregular

about	front	their
also	live	through
always	other	would

Challenge Words

between	finally	moving	protection	swamps
capybara	minute	prefer	record	
enemy	mostly	preferred	submarine	

Now that you have met the jaguar, it might be a good time to meet one more temperate forest animal: the capybara.

Capybaras are rodents,

but don't think for a minute
that they seem like rats
or mice. A full-grown
capybara can tip the scales
at 175 pounds!

Capybaras like to crawl

about and play in water-
rich parts of tropical
forests. They prefer to
stay in marshes, bogs,
rivers, and swamps. These
places offer good food as

well as protection.

Capybaras feast on tough reeds, grasses, and other plants. This could cause their teeth to get dull. But did you know that

the capybara's front teeth
never stop growing? They
are always on point and
ready to saw their way
through plants and twigs.
Water is a good place

to hide when the capybara
is hunted. It has grown
so that its eyes, ears, and
nose are close to the top of
its head. That means the
capybara can stay mostly

underwater with just the
smallest part of it able to
be seen. If it stays low and
still, and makes no noise,
most enemies will miss it.
But if it *is* seen, a

capybara has webs
between its toes that help
it swim out of sight quickly.
It can also hold its breath
under water for a long
time. Even a jaguar that

can swim would find it
hard to keep up with the
capybara when it is playing
at being a submarine.

Finally, capybaras like
to live and sleep in packs.

They protect each other, if needed, with warnings when an enemy comes close. They also help each other reach the plants they like to eat.

When you are a

175-pound rodent, you need a lot of food, so it is good to have a team!

Animal Corner. (n.d.). *Hedgehog.* https://animalcorner.org/animals/
hedgehog/

The Editors of Encyclopaedia Britannica. (2025, July 31). *Capybara.*
https://www.britannica.com/animal/capybara-genus

The Environmental Literacy Council. (2025, May 3). *What traits help
capybaras survive?* https://enviroliteracy.org/what-traits-help-
capybaras-survive/

National Geographic Kids. (n.d.). *Hedgehog facts!* https://www.
natgeokids.com/uk/discover/animals/general-animals/hedgehog-
facts/

Cat Jenkins lives in the Pacific Northwest where the weather is often conducive to long hours before a keyboard. Her stories in humor, fantasy, speculative fiction and horror have been published both online and in print.

Storyshares is focused on supporting older striving readers by creating a new shelf in the library specifically for them. The ever-growing collection features content that is compelling and culturally relevant for older students, teens, and adults, yet still readable at a range of lower reading levels.

Storyshares generates content by engaging deeply with writers, bringing together a community to create this new kind of book. With more intriguing and approachable stories to choose from, striving readers are improving their skills and beginning to discover the joy of reading. For more information, visit storyshares.org.

Easy to Read. Hard to Put Down.